Carambola

Carambola

Poems by Shayla Hawkins

David Robert Books

Published by David Robert Books
P.O. Box 541106
Cincinnati, OH 45254-1106

ISBN: 9781625490018
LCCN: 2012953027

Poetry Editor: Kevin Walzer
Business Editor: Lori Jareo

Visit us on the web at www.davidrobertbooks.com

To God, for the power and beauty of language,

and to poetry, for giving me a seat at the table

Grateful acknowledgment is made to the editors of the following publications in which these poems (sometimes in earlier versions) first appeared:

African Voices: "Jemima"

Aunt Chloe: "When Aretha Sang 'Mary, Don't You Weep'"

Pembroke Magazine: "Oh, Brownie"

Pyrta: "Carambola" and "My Beloved's Voice"

Quantum Leap: "Polvorones"

Solo Café 8&9: "The Seed"

St. Somewhere: "Cuba Night Woman" and "Cyan Blue"

Taj Mahal Review: "Nilgiri Tea"

The Poetry Church: "Michelangelo's Pietá"

Torch: Poetry, Prose, and Short Stories by African American Women: "Nest of Honey: A Blues for Samson"

Vwa: Poems for Haiti: "Visionary"

Table of Contents

I.

The Seed

My first teacher: my mother
My first school desk: her lap

My first English, science and geography
lessons: the books she read to me
and taught me to read for myself

Her larger, stronger fingers guiding mine
through page after page of squiggly black
lines,

sounding each one slowly
until the strange dark marks,
coupled with my understanding,
cleared like a sea mist

and became words that opened
like curtains and doors
into worlds of pirates and fairies,
reindeer and sugar plums,
poison apples and gingerbread houses

My mother's voice conjuring
from paper and ink
tales of prophets and pharaohs,
princesses and shepherd kings

Her patient, persistent teaching
igniting my mind,
planting the seed of a passion
that would erupt and soar
like a fairytale beanstalk

to the heavens

The Day I Stopped Being Afraid of Thunder

It slammed against the house
like a demon's fist,
shook the floor,
and sent me flying
to my parents' bedroom.

My father,
who refused to let a thunderstorm
interrupt his sleep,
rested soundly,
his snores softening
the jagged edge of the night.
My mother,
who was wise
even at three o'clock
in the morning,
smoothed my ponytail and said,
"Thunder is loud,
but it can't hurt you.
It's the quiet lightning
you should be scared of."

Huddled inside my mother's arms
during those dark hours,
I stared into the flashing night,

forever changed
by the sly, absolute power of silence.

Love

My mother did not pity me
the day I had my wisdom teeth removed.
She did not panic
at the sight of my swollen face.
She did not crumble
when I crouched in the bathroom
like a useless thing
and spat blood and pus into the toilet.
My mother did not lullaby my pain.

But in the world between sleeping and waking,
I saw my mother's soft shadow slide
through the newness of morning,
stand in silence over my bed.
I heard the cushioned hush
of her car as it carried her
through the chilled February air.

My mother brought the cure quietly:
She put a bottle of penicillin in my hand
and called me to the kitchen.
She had prepared a bowl of grits with butter
and pepper,
a meal that could be received easily
by my freshly torn gums.

I sat at the table and ate,
the smooth grains of my mother's love
sliding down my throat
like petitioned rain.

Autopsy

I.

My father grabs my hand.
I feel the smooth skin
under his thumb,
the steady tick of his pulse.
He looks ahead, steps down,
his face a waning moon
among shadows.

We are in the Wayne County Morgue,
descending to the basement
where forensic vans
unload the dead,
where women and men like my father
use scissors, saws, and knives
to dissect the difference
between living and dying.

Dad leads me forward,
our arms a chain stretching through the dark,
our feet a soft thunder on the stairs.
He squeezes my fingers, asks if I'm afraid.
I squeeze back and say no.
We reach the bottom.
My father opens a door, nudges me ahead.

A wave of white light floods my face.
The truth is I am more frightened than I know.
But my fear will have to wait.
My father is teaching me *autopsy*:
to see with my own eyes.
My father is teaching me to live.

II.

The first corpse
is a black man.
The skin above his chest
parted like wings
or the flaps
of a fragile door.
Lower, his spleen,
beige pouch of stomach,
the pink gleam of intestines,
vivid and elegant,
curled and stacked
on top of each other
like a litter
of newborn animals.

He lies on the metal table,
head propped, mouth gaping
as if on the verge
of telling a secret
he can't keep to himself.
The faucet at his feet
drips like a liquid clock,
his toe tag: a pendulum.

III.

Dr. Taylor is so busy laughing with my father
over last night's Pistons game
that he does not notice me
or the way his latexed fingers
unclench the brain he has just removed
from a female cadaver.

As he and Daddy bask in the vicarious glory
of Isaiah Thomas's jump shots,
Dr. Taylor plops the fleshy ball onto a scale.
The brain rolls in the silver pan,
then stops and stands
quiet as an obedient child.

Were it possible,
I would step through the unseen door
that divides me
from the woman who housed this brain
to ask what she feels
now that the keeper and creator
of her bigotries and dreams
has been reduced
to this dry, coiled gray mass.

I bend and peer into the dark hollow
of her skull. It looks like a shell,
and, to test my theory,

I whisper *Hello.*

I swear the sound curves along the bone
and sends back to my ears
a chorus of echoes and sighs
that lift and vanish like a rush of wind
dissolving in endless space.

II.

Nest of Honey: A Blues for Samson

after Luca Giordano's painting Samson and the Lion

"…and Samson turned aside to see the carcass of the
lion: and, behold, there was a swarm of bees and honey
in the carcass of the lion." — Judges 14:8

I killed a lion with my hands, yanked its mouth
'til it was torn;
Said I killed a lion with my bare hands 'til its
jaw was bloody and torn.
That lion died such an awful death, it cursed
the day it was born.

With the strength in my hair,
I turned that lion into a hive of bees;
Said I went to that lair and turned that lion's
corpse to a nest of honey for the bees.
But I had no clue a bee named Delilah was
about to come and sting *me*.

That woman Delilah put a spell on me and I let
her in my bed.
Her body was tight, she loved me right and I
put her in my bed.
Then she called the Philistines to put out my
eyes and cut the hair off my head.

She ripped my heart like I ripped that lion
and brought me to my knees;
Said Delilah was the poison that killed my
power and brought me to my knees.
She turned my body into a corpse
and a nest of honey for the bees.

Bathsheba's Shower

On her skin, water wasn't just water;
it was a bright and wild and living thing.
In that moment, she was not wife or daughter:
She was beautiful, naked, and I was king.

I ignored all I knew of wrong and right,
of God and salvation and Satan and sin.
Bewitched by that wet woman in my sight,
I fed my carnal craving and called her in.

What did I know then of God's great anger
when I lured Bathsheba to my bed?
Drunk with her flesh and blind to the danger,
how could I care for her husband soon dead?

Or know our first son was born for the grave?
So costly the lust that makes a king a slave.

Reuben's Mandrakes

And Reuben went in the days of wheat harvest and found mandrakes in the field, and brought them to his mother Leah. Then Rachel said to Leah, "Give me, I pray thee, of thy son's mandrakes." But Leah said to her, "Is it a small matter that thou hast taken my husband? Wouldest thou take away my son's mandrakes also?" And Rachel said, "Therefore he shall lie with thee tonight for your son's mandrakes." When Jacob came out of the field in the evening, Leah went out to meet him and said, "Thou must come in to me, for I have surely hired thee with my son's mandrakes." And he lay with her that night.
– Genesis 30:14-16

To draw you to my bed,
this is what it takes:
A word from my sister,
and our son's mandrakes.

You came to my tent,
my body's thirst to slake
only after I traded you
for Reuben's mandrakes.

For your caress on my starved skin,
this love and passion you fake,
I have paid dearly with my tears,

your distance,
and the beguiling roots
of Reuben's mandrakes.

Jemima

*So the Lord blessed the latter end of Job more than his
beginning … He also had seven sons and three
daughters. And he called the name of the first Jemima,
the name of the second Kezia, and the name of the third
Kerenhappuch. In all the land were no women found so
beautiful as the daughters of Job…. – Job 42:12-15*

Before my name was blended
with cornbread mix and pancake batter,
Before I wore head rags
that mummified my hair,

Before America twisted me
into the paradox of a fat woman
who cooks but never eats,
who breastfeeds babies but never has sex,

Before I became the maid
who never goes home
and has nothing better to do
with her time or possibilities
than smile like an idiot
and scrub a white person's kitchen,

Before I was anybody's aunt,
I was Job's daughter,

the promise after his punishment,
the sunlight after his sorrow

My hair was lush and thick
as the ferns that grew in my father's garden,
my voice clear and sweet as honey,
my skin the color of Egyptian sand,
my body tender as a water lily

Men rode camels for days to reach me
and bathed my feet
with their drinking water

And I grew into a beautiful woman
who walked in wisdom
and brought love to her world
without a mop, broom, or pancake
in sight

When Aretha Sang "Mary, Don't You Weep"

Greater Emmanuel C.O.G.I.C., June 15, 2007,
Detroit, MI

You could hear bones
and the surge of blood and chains
in that music

You could feel the salt spray of the Atlantic,
the rhythmic rocking of slave ships
that held in their putrid holds
shackled tribes of the Duala,
Fulani, Mandinka, Igbo, Isubu, Ashanti

And when Aretha hit the high note
of her climax,
when she said "Lazarus" that third time,
her voice rose and thundered
like the Shekinah Glory,
that whirlwind of shadow and fire
that shielded the Israelites from their
would-be Egyptian killers

Aretha's voice unleashed
and became the Red Sea
crashing down on Pharaoh's warriors

Anyone who was in that sanctuary that night
could tell you that when Aretha sang,
the floor and the windows
shook as if Jesus himself
had hurled the devil back to Hell
for the very last time,

like the stone holding Lazarus
in his grave was rolling back,
so that Lazarus, hearing his name,
could obey the command
of his resurrection
and walk into the miracle and majesty
and the second chance of his life

Michelangelo's Pietá

His vision a hunger,
his hands, an urgent clock,
strike blank stone.
Invisible beasts guide him,
bless his cramped fingers,
his crown of glistening sweat.
Blizzards of dust and jagged rock
fill the air.
He pounds and shatters
until the stone breathes,
releases a mother
who knows nothing of angels or grace,
feels only the dead weight of her child.

She hears voices call him Messiah,
but his blood clings to her like a shroud.
Liquid salt stings her eyes.
She does not know about faith
or the artist who, like her son,
will give resurrection to this death,
prove that stone can obey,
that sometimes even God
needs a resting place.

Lessons of the Poppies

after Georgia O'Keefe's Oriental Poppies

Know
your season
Honor
your rhythm

Awaken
at the appointed time
with the slow
radiant power
of a world
called from darkness
into life's blood and fire

Unfurl
your heart
with a petal's
exotic grace

Let the mysterious
dark of your beginnings
sing and lure you like a siren
through your soul's
flaming ethereal
doors

Grace

after Henry Ossawa Tanner's The Thankful Poor

For reaching down through time
and bestowing the bread and drink at this table

For replacing the sweat and dust
of our daily lives
with a clean and ready pitcher,
cups and plates

For giving us a place in this world
where we can be not servants of others,

outcast and despised for the color of our skin,
but men in our own right,
formed in your image,

For giving us a moment where we,
young and old,
can nourish our bodies and rest our souls,

We praise your great mercy
and thank you, O Lord,
for feeding us from the fullness of your earth.

Bass Ackwards

after Marc Chagall's The Birthday

Look what your love made me do:
Tie on my cup, drink from my shoe
fly off the bed, roll through the air
comb my teeth, floss my hair
make me hear cows quack
and ducks say "Moo"
Look what your love has made me do

Look how your birthday made me act,
like a leapfrog and a caffeinated acrobat
like an airborne snake, like a flying fish
that flipped its head backwards
to give you a kiss,
like a dead man risen
from his cold, lonely grave
Oh, look how your birthday
has made me behave

III.

Fish Vocabulary

Last week at the mall,
I heard a woman ask her friend:
"So when are you two getting married?"
The other woman said,
"I don't know, girl, but I've got him hooked,
and I'm doing my best to reel him in!"

They laughed. Silently, I laughed, too,
amused that a woman
could think of a man like he's a fish,
as though he could be baited like a tuna,
trapped and sautéed like a trout.

I prayed that day that if I ever meet a man
I want to marry,
I won't need fish vocabulary
to describe him,
that my love for him
will be as deep and mysterious as the oceans,
that his kisses will be
tender as a dolphin's skin,
that his love and lust for me
will come as natural
as a flounder's need
to find the open sea.

Polvorones

for Alana

My co-worker has brought two trays
of Mexican wedding cookies to share.

She calls them *polvorones*, dusty things,
and explains that the cakes are named
for their thin coating of confectioners' sugar.

I take one and notice how
each piece is powdered
with the sweet, white dust
and looks for all the world
like a face behind a wedding veil.

I unclench the cookie and it rolls
to the center of my palm,
a small heavy circle,
a world unto itself.

And this, I think, as I bite into the *polvoron*
and its crunchy mélange
of cinnamon, vanilla and pecan
melt into my tongue,
this is how I want my marriage to be:
a little nutty,
sweet but salty enough

to stay interesting,
filled with good things
that grow better
when tried by fire,
taken from the dust
and crafted with care
into a solid, perfect sphere
without end.

Veneer

Hollywood actor/director unleashes profanity-laced
phone tirade at mistress, punches veneers off her two
front teeth – Entertainment news report

On my TV again the latest tired tale
of a woman who thought
adultery's trick dice
would roll in her favor
but was smacked back
to reality by the married lover
no longer tantalized with her body
who now feels trapped
and betrayed and wants her gone,
who ripped the glitzy façade
off their Hollywood happiness
as powerfully as he punched
the veneers out of her mouth

Before her first whim
to ride a famous man to glory,
Before her first plane trip to Los Angeles,
old girl would have done well to stopover
in some sleepy Mississippi or Carolina town
where the old school church ladies
and grandmothers would have sat her down
at a creaky wood table,

tucked a paper napkin in her blouse
and fed her a hot, heaping plate of wisdom
along with cornbread and smothered chicken,
apple cobbler and mustard greens

They would have told her
with no nonsense that you don't play house
with another woman's husband,
that you don't have to steal
what is truly yours,
that there is no wealth or power
so great as knowing your worth,
loving the work
of your own hands,
and tasting the sweetness
of your own name
in your own mouth

The Vanishing

A car appeared at the end
of my street one morning.
It looked comfortable on the concrete,
as though it had always been there.
But the longer that car stayed,
the lesser it became.

A day later,
it was propped on four cinder blocks,
tires gone.
The next day, the doors were missing.
By that night,
the seats, bumper, and fender
had vanished.
The next morning,
the car's hood was lifted,
engine gutted,
windows and windshields
smashed.

That afternoon, the cinder blocks
and what was left of that car
were towed away.
For weeks, I remembered it
and marveled at the people

who had stripped that car so completely,
no one, not even its owner,
would recognize it.

In sad wonder I shook my head,
because I knew
that those thieves' destruction
could never have been so potent
had they not first
practiced it on themselves.

He Gathers Sweet Potatoes

St. Philip's Parish, Barbados

He walks this field today
as he has walked it thousands of times:
surely, carefully, fearlessly.

He and the land are so intimate,
they are starting to look alike:
his dull white shirt mimics
the low, heavy clouds
trimmed with gray.
His brown skin and pants
have become extensions
of the earth that he owns,
that owns him.

The green leaves of a sweet potato crop
have risen from the dirt under his feet.
Like the horizon,
they stretch far beyond his body.

His fingers clasp the cloth bag
that drags behind him.
He does not seem to fight or question
his need for this sweetness
or the sweat it requires.

He simply yields to it,
like the leafless tree
that towers over him
and has learned
to bend to the earth
and tolerate its gravity
without breaking.

Cyan Blue

Nassau, Bahamas

the old man
points me
down George Street
to the pirate museum

his fingers gnarled
and brown as a banyan tree
hair
ocean foam silver
eyes
wild cyan blue

already showing me
the rebel beauty
I'll see in the wax figures
of Anne Bonny
Captain Teach
Calico Jack

this old man's
earth dark skin
and seawater eyes
 Carib yin-yang
of duppy and angel
bondservant and buccaneer

the Bahamian brew
of his African and European blood
braided smooth as the dreadlocks
on Blackbeard's face

Rio de Janeiro Blue

The DJ calls it
"music for the grown folks,"
and with a welcome reprieve
from the hyper-sexed,
over-synthesized hip hop
and gangsta rappers
dropping crime-laced rhymes
like bullets,

The radio delivers
Randy Crawford's quicksilver vibrato,
her voice bright and smooth
as the equatorial moon,
taking the blueprint
of lyrics, guitar, flute and cabasa,
turning them to sky, sand,
water and stone

A city painted into sound through her song:
the Atlantic's ceaseless turquoise tongue
licking the Copacabana shore

Christ the Redeemer
and its chiseled rock arms stretched
like wings over Rio,
a beacon to the city's legions of poor,

hidden in plain sight
just beyond the mountains

Brazil's color and rhythm
bathed in the cool blue flame
of one woman's voice,
Rio's carnival air,
its Samba and lusty flash
converted through her arias
into rhapsody and beautiful desolation

Cuba Night Woman

After dark
I slide
like a serpent
out of my skin

and become
the blue bahía
of Cienfuegos

the rhythm
and orishas of Rumba

the sugar-sweet smoke
of Cohíba curling
vanishing
like a spirit
in the wet-hot
Havana night

the crocodile's
lash and bite

the fever blood
of lovers
that could call fire
from rain

Come daylight
I am woman
again

Postcard from Mt. Fuji, Japan

In the land
of Nagasaki and Hiroshima
where the sky once rained fire
and changed children, women and men
into cinders and smoky wisps
of flesh,

Now a picture of peace,
a moment of stillness
beauty and life

The once flaming sea of air
now filled with the cherry blossom's
soft pink explosions,
now cooled by the quiet lake
and the mountain
with its imperial crown of snow

Old Cousin Ethel: A Bop

Old Cousin Ethel
had a heavy load husband
who used to do her wrong.
He came home at sunup
and he would beat her
after staying out drunk all night long.

Old Cousin Ethel lost her heavy load
one summer night along a Carolina road.

She grabbed a shovel one evening
while he was sleeping in the bed.
And that heavy load husband
never felt that heavy metal
come crashing down on his head.
Then Ethel got dressed in her Sunday best,
drove her problem to the swamp,
and let the gators do the rest.

Old Cousin Ethel lost her heavy load
one summer night along a Carolina road.

The church folk gossiped
about what happened to that man,
but none of them could say for sure.
All they knew was one night,

he tipped out of sight
and never again darkened Ethel's door.

Old Cousin Ethel lost her heavy load
one summer night along a Carolina road.

Oh, Brownie

*In a failed attempt to show control in the catastrophic
aftermath of Hurricane Katrina, President George W.
Bush scheduled a media stop at the Mobile Regional
Airport in Mobile, Alabama, on Friday, September 2,
2005. The photo op produced one of the most criticized
quotes of Bush's presidency. As news cameras rolled,
Bush told Michael Brown, director of the Federal
Emergency Management Agency, "Brownie, you're
doing a heck of a job." But Brown and FEMA were
roundly lambasted for their ineptitude and
incomprehensibly slow response in sending help to the
thousands of dying, starving and homeless residents in
New Orleans and throughout the Gulf region. Brown,
furthermore, had no prior emergency management
experience and just four years earlier had worked as
commissioner of the International Arabian Horse
Association. The irony and absurdity of Bush's praise
became all the more glaring when Brown, under
mounting pressure, resigned as FEMA director just 10
days later.*

I've flown to this Alabama townie
To praise you, my good yes-man Brownie,
Though there's talk you don't have a clue
About what you should do,
And the media calls you a clownie.

You're not skilled in hurricanes but horsies.

Maybe that's why FEMA's off-coursie
And why Katrina victims say
Instead of taking pain away,
You're making it far much worsie.

Today I've got your back, Brownie,
So don't you be worried or frownie –
But if this train wreck we see
Ever points back to me,
Then on your sword I'll make you fall downie!

IV.

Your Body is a Temple

Your body is a temple and I have come to pray,
to bathe in your soul's perfect light,
to leave in your arms the stress of this day.
Your body is a temple and I have come to pray,
to feel the blessed touch that casts my fears away,
to taste the sacred kiss that makes all things right.
Your body is a temple and I have come to pray,
to bathe in your soul's perfect light.

Nilgiri Tea

Tender as the night in Trivandrum
your shadow steals over me,
secret and dark like the new moon,
soothing as Nilgiri tea

One look at you and my soul lifts
like the salt-rimmed waves of the sea.
My heart grows enthused like water infused
with the black leaves of Nilgiri tea

When I surrender to sleep's deep calm,
and in dreams my inhibition flies free,
then you slip softest into my body,
sleek and warm as Nilgiri tea

Brahma

Brahma is the Hindu god (deva) of creation ... and is traditionally depicted with four heads and four faces and four arms. – Wikipedia

for Sendhil

I wish I had the four hands of Brahma
so I could use twenty fingers to spin
an invisible web of pleasure
along the copper brown swales of your skin

I wish I had the four heads of Brahma
so I could shout from my four mouths
the bliss of beholding your comeliness
from the east, west, north and south

My Beloved's Voice

a haiku

Masculine music
A lion in the lilies
The sun wrapped in clouds

Calypso Orchid

His lips string a strand
of kisses around her neck

His breath a sea breeze
on her shoulders

And her skin,
what used to be mere bandage
for her bones,
blooms with heat and blood

She transforms under his touch
into a calypso orchid
lush, vibrant, wild

Carambola

soft
as air
on my skin

some incorporeal hand
reaches
through the night

lifts open
my sleeping eyes
guides them
to the warmth
of your fingers
splayed
across my waist
like a fan

some gentle
unconscious claim
of possession
that circuits
your mind
even as you slumber

your hand
a sweet carambola

on my body,
a rugged
five-point star
that tethers us
to each other
glides us
across
the witching hours
to morning's
bright and open door

Mosquito

She rides the night,
heedless of nothing
save the desire
restless, dark and sly as herself

Pulled by thirst and a passion
more ancient than the moon,
she finds me,
my body's flame-red glow and heat
as bright to her eyes
as a flare shot into the twilight

Quiet as a wish,
she drifts down,
straddles my skin
then pricks and plunges
her tongue into my arm,
her secret itch now my own
as she sips the small pearl of blood
that bubbles from my vein
with the grace of a countess
sipping her chalice of wine,

until, sated, she floats away
into the moist, hot night

The bump on my arm rises
I stare at the sky and wonder
how far she will go,
how far she will carry me
in her bite,
in her blood

Night Fisher

Your embrace
full as an ocean
sealing me
in its liquid skin

Your hand
a bluepoint knife
sliding open my legs

And you
a night fisher
casting the nets
of your fingers
over me

Until
glittering wet
as an oyster
lifted from the deep

The soft shell
of my flesh
cracks and spills
its salt-sweet musk over you
like the twilight's rain
into the sea

Twenty Romans

after Stevie Smith's "Tenuous and Precarious"

Calamitous and Arduous
were my early life.
Arduous and Calamitous,
Two Romans.

Avaricious, Mendacious and Treacherous
were my former bosses.
Mendacious, Treacherous, Avaricious.
Five Romans.

Hilarious and Ridiculous
were my paychecks.
Ridiculous and Hilarious,
Seven Romans.

Noxious, Hazardous and Preposterous
were my past suitors.
Preposterous. Noxious. Hazardous.
Ten Romans.

But then I became
Adventurous and Audacious.
Audacious and Adventurous I grew.
Twelve Romans.

And met a man
who is Equanimous, Gorgeous and Gracious.
Gracious, Equanimous and Gorgeous.
Fifteen Romans.

His love, like his kisses,
Sumptuous, Copious, Delicious.
Copious, Sumptuous, Delicious.
Eighteen Romans.

My life today is,
like a sultan's riches,

Bounteous and Auspicious.
Twenty Romans.

Brie and Cabernet

At an art gallery
a man, handsome and sleek,
strides to a table of silver trays
filled with wine and cheese

He lifts a small knife
that gleams like glass
against his skin,
cuts a wedge from
the soft, exotic Brie,
spreads it over a wafer
slides it into his mouth
with such deliberation and grace
that I, watching at a distance,
can almost taste the cheese,
its smooth, buttery zest
on his tongue,
almost smell the rich notes
of vanilla, oak and spice
in the glass of cabernet
he lifts to his lips and drinks

I can almost see the wine's fluid face
slip into his mouth
like the heat and breath
of a woman's kiss

and I imagine that man,
later that night, sleeping,
cabernet still warming his flesh,
dreams ascending his mind
unlocking his desires,
stirring his blood like wine

Salt Lick

Just for tonight
forget my name

Call me Adam's Rib

Taste my tender skin
formed from your own flesh

Let the slow burn of your hands,
the salt lick of your tongue
bathe me
the way meat
washes clean
in fire

Savor the sweaty glaze of my skin

Wrap yourself in me
the way the blazing
summer night
swells thick with hickory
and binds the wind
with its fragrant, lacy steam

Venus Ascending

an alabaster moon
hangs in the August night:
a polished pearl
in Othello's ear

ancient legions
of crickets and cicadas
call from the grass and trees
singing away
the day's pathos

and in my candlelit bath
I am an island
and woman
of my own making
the water a rose-scented sea
softening the shores of my skin

at my cleansing's end
I rise through mist
and fragrant foam
like Venus ascending
the Mediterranean's
liquid multitudes:
whole, beautiful and free

V.

Compassion: A Triolet

in memory of Tonia Carmichael, Nancy Cobbs, Tishana
Culver, Crystal Dozier, Telacia Fortson, Amelda Hunter,
LeShanda Long, Michelle Mason, Kim Yvette Smith,
Diane Turner, and Janice Webb, murdered from 2007 to
2009 by Anthony Sowell at his house on Imperial
Avenue in Cleveland, Ohio

What does it take to hear a black woman scream,
to save her from a cold, violent death?
How long must she bleed before her bruises are seen?
What does it take to hear a black woman scream?
How long will she be the target of a killer's dream
and terror's pain steal her last breath?
What does it take to hear a black woman scream,
to save her from a cold, violent death?

Passion Blessed

for Michael Jackson

Sweat pouring
like rain from his face,
dripping down his hair
like diamonds

The stadium crowd
a human sea,
Their claps and cheers
a palpable thunder

And Michael
standing on stage,
eyes closed, chest heaving,
oblivious to the cameras,
the spotlight, the screaming

In this moment
the definition of a man
who has given his all,
whose slim, fragile body
has smashed the barrier
between dance and divinity,
song and the sacred,
whose spins and twists,
torques and slides

have straddled the gap between
the known and the impossible
and redefined the rhythm
of the human form

In this moment completely
and yet more than himself,
not just a performer,
but a vessel, a purpose,
a passion blessed
and filled
to overflowing

Visionary

for Franck Louissaint, Levoy Exil, Georges Nader Jr.,
and all keepers and creators of Haitian art

a prophet
this painter
who saw
with his brush
and canvas
what his mind
could not know:

a woman
her brown skin
illumined like a tree
in the Haitian sun,
her face shaded
by two heavy bags
of American rice
she carries
stacked like pillows
atop her head,
her gaze calm,
a captivating glance
at a warrior
walking the thin line
between relief
and disaster

an oracle
this other painter
who saw
in the blood-red
and crypt-dark colors
of his work
Haiti's colossus of death
and shattering
one year
before it came

for these
and all the visual poets
who foresaw
the destruction
and changed it
to a beautiful agony,
a living testimony,
for the gallery
and museum owners
who chose to stay
and salvage
what they can
of a nation's
crumbled history,

may their visions
of healing and restoration
be fulfilled,

may their art
give back
to the Haitian people
not a miracle
not false, easy hope
but a true knowing
of their strength,
a solid faith
that, if they cannot
escape trouble
and pain,
they will, at least,
be able to lift
and carry
those burdens
like sacks of American rice
on their heads

Strong Medicine

for Lucille Clifton, June 27, 1936-February 13, 2010

i am summoned
this day
to the genesis and revelation
of my name: light

after 73 years,
i leave the healing,
strong medicine
of my words
as the rain
offers its kiss
to a field of lilies
as a mother
hugs her children
when they leave for school

after 73 years,
i am led to this:
love's abyss
and its everlasting embrace

and so i shake off
my snowy crown of hair
my brown, battle-weary body

and with my last breath
i surrender
and ride my light
into the starry, endless sea
of worlds
and time

I thank wholeheartedly the following:

All my great mentors and teachers, especially
Mrs. Thelma Dinwiddie, Ms. Patricia Leslie,
Mrs. Brendolyn McClain, Mr. Dudley Randall,
Ms. Jamie Tobin, Elder Edward Summerville,
and Dr. Charles Johnson, each of whom
predicted, and encouraged, my book writing
career;

my parents, Shirley and Edward, who got the
ball rolling;

Samuel Johnson and my brother Donny, for
their unconditional kindness, support, and
splendid humanity;

Lenard Moore and Willie Williams, for their
time and their faith in my first book;

my poetry teachers at Cave Canem, and the
staffs of the Poetry at Noon series at the
Library of Congress and the Geraldine R.
Dodge Poetry Festival;

and, above all, the Lord Jesus Christ, for
having a greater vision for me than I had for
myself, and for the incredible gifts and
privileges of love, art, life, and Grace Amazing.

S. H.

CPSIA information can be obtained at www.ICGtesting.com
Printed in the USA
BVOW020156211112

306083BV00001B/36/P